Red Books *showing the way*

LOCAL STREET ATLAS

C000120127

HARROGATE
KNARESBOROUGH

FOLLIFOOT · GATES HILL · HAMPSTHWAITE
KILLINGHALL · SPOFFORTH · PANNAL

CONTENTS

LEGEND

	Pedestrianized / Restricted Access
	Track
	Built Up Area
– – – –	Footpath
	Stream
	River
Lock	Canal
	Railway / Station
●	Post Office
P P+	Car Park / Park & Ride
C	Public Convenience
✛	Place of Worship
→	One-way Street
i	Tourist Information Centre
▲8 ▲8	Adjoining Pages
	Area Depicting Enlarged Centre
	Emergency Services
	Industrial Buildings
	Leisure Buildings
	Education Buildings
	Hotels etc.
	Retail Buildings
	General Buildings
	Woodland
	Orchard
	Recreational / Parkland
	Cemetery

Every effort has been made to verify the accuracy of information in this book but the publishers cannot accept responsibility for expense or loss caused by an error or omission.

Information that will be of assistance to the user of the maps will be welcomed.

The representation on these maps of a road, track or path is no evidence of the existence of a right of way.

Street plans prepared and published by
Red Books (Estate Publications) Ltd, Bridewell House, Tenterden, Kent, TN30 6EP.
The Publishers acknowledge the co-operation of the local authorities of towns represented in this atlas.

 Ordnance Survey® This product includes mapping data licensed from Ordnance Survey® with the permission of the Controller of Her Majesty's Stationery Office.

© Crown Copyright
© Red Books (Estate Publications) Ltd

ISBN 978-1-84192-365-9
635-02/06-04

All rights reserved
Licence Number 100019031

www.redbooks-maps.co.uk

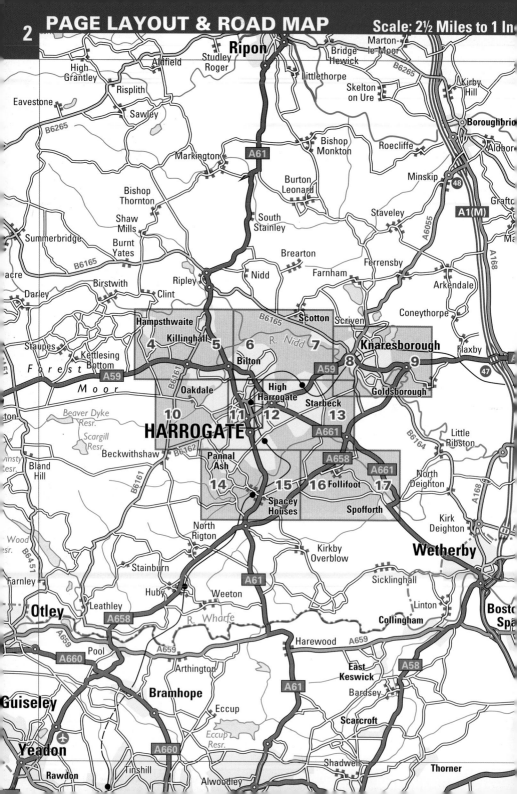

HAMPSTHWAITE

A **B** **C** **D**

1

River Nidd

Sewage Farm

School

2

Hampsthwaite

PECKFIELD CL

HIGH

MEADOW CL

ROWDEN LANE

CHURCH LANE

STREET

FINDEN GDNS

BROOKFIELD CLOSE

BROOKFIELD WY

BROOKFIELD GARTH

BROOKFIELD

DALE CLOSE

HOLLINS

HOLLINS CL

BARTON CT

Knox Hill

3

Hollins Farm

Hampsthwaite Hollins

WEST CT

EAST CT

GARDEN CT

HOLLINS HALL ST

LODGE ST

HOLLINS LANE

LANE

ROWDEN

Barton House

CHAIN BAR LANE

LUND LANE

LEVENS HALL

PARK

LEVENS CL

MYGAS GREEN LANE

LA

4

Rowden

WEST LANE

Shutt Nook Farm

Saltergate Hill

5

A59

SKIPTON RD

SKIPTON

BURLEY BANK ROAD

Dike Bottom Farm

Saltergate Beck

ROA

Travel Rest F

R O A

6

Burley Bank Farm

Heather House Farm

OAKER

B6161

BUTTER

NK

ST

P

A **B** **C** **D**

10

E   **F**   **G**   **H**

Scotton

SCOTTON CT
LANE
HAVIKIL PK
MIRE SYKE LANE
HAVIKIL
ST JOHNS RD
NEW
Rec Grnd
HIGH
Scotton Park Caravan Site
RIPLEY
ROAD
ROAD
ge
SCOTTON GRO
SCOTTON DR
SCOTTON DR
P
RIPLEY
MOOR LANE
RED HILL LANE

Preston House

Low Preston Covert

1

Gates Hill
Appleby Carr
2
WAL
PRESTON BOTTOMS LANE
GAKER
8
Coalpits Wood
River Nidd
Bilton Banks
Oak Bank
Jack Carter's Cave
APPLEBY GRN
APPLEBY GRO
APPLEBY
APPLEBY WY
AVENUE
APPLEBY
APPLEBY GATE
APPLEBY AVE
APPLEBY
APPLEBY CT
NETHEREDGE
NETHER EDGE
FORTUNE DR
HILL
FORTUNE
HILL
ROAD
B6165
B6165
3
LANDS
LANE
NIDD
BA

Scotton Banks
Spring Wood
Caravan & Camping Site
BILTON
Fox Wood
Weir

Limekiln Plantation
Bilton Hall
LANE
Harrogate Ringway
4
Co
8

BILTON HALL DRIVE
A59
HEAD
5
OG

College
THE DRIVE
ROAD
BOGS
Forest Head Farm
FOREST
LANE
HEAD
HA
Belmont Wood

Kingsley Farm
KINGSLEY
DIAMOND GRO
DIAMOND PL
VICTORIA
THE
HARRISON GRO
REGENT PL
PEARL ST
REGENT
MT
REGENT
ST
HILLBANK VW
HILLBANK GRO
HILLBANK
HIGHBANK GRO
LANE
FOREST
MAPLE
MILLFIELD GLADE
Club House

Rec Grnd
AVENUE
LAUNDRY
Harrogate Golf Course
6

ROAD
DRIVE
KINGSLEY
OLIVE GRO
OLIVE
WY
OLIVE WALK
F'ball nd
12
STATIO
ALBERT PL
STREETE
STREET
FOREST
LANE
HEAD
A59
MOORLAND RD
Forest Lane Head
MOORLAND
VW
WORT
ST
MOORLAND
School
13
Knaresboro Round

E   **F**   **G**   **H**

E   F   G   H

Mill Farm

Hay-a-Park

Castle Farm

1

Hall Farm

Oakwood Farm

2

GRO

WTONDALE

Highfield House

3

A59

R O A D

Y O R K

ELD

PDALE

RAY-A-

SDALE

CL

Manse Farm

ASHWOOD PL

ALDER AV

NIDDERDALE

LODGE PARK

Caravan Park

R O A D

Y O R K

Goldsborough Fields

4

MANSE LANE
INDUSTRIAL
ESTATE

Sewage Works

R O A D

Burial Ground

NKSWELL

Goldsborough
Cricket
Club

5

ST JAMES
BUSINESS &
RETAIL PARK

River Nidd

GRIMBALD CRAG

GRIMBALD CRAG RD

School

EAST
VIEW

CT

Goldsborough

CHURCH
ST

CHURCH STREET

WOODLAND
CL

S T A T I O N

P R I N C E S S

M E A D

BROUGH
CT

MBALD

CRAG
WY

HERBY
RD

AVENUE
HOUSE
ROAD

CT

MIDGELEY

Lido
van
k

WETHERBY RD B6164

Goldsborough Mill
Farm

M I L L

R O A D   M I L L

Goldsborough Park

6

A658

E   F   G   H

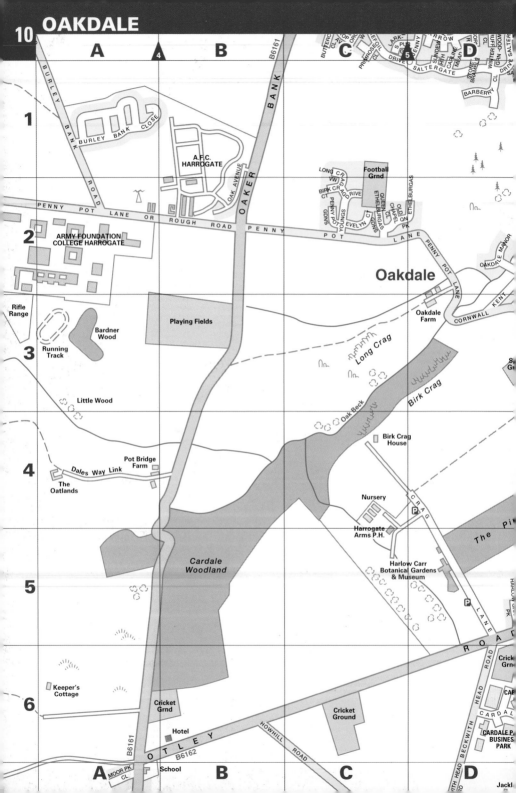

A map page showing Oakdale area with grid references A–D and 1–6.

A **B** B6161 **C** **D**

BURLEY BANK ROAD

BURLEY BANK CLOSE

A.F.C. HARROGATE

OAK AVENUE

OAKER BANK

Football Grnd

LONG CRAG
VW
BIRK CRAG CT
RIVE
PENNY POT GDNS
SONYCA
QUEEN CHAPEL
ETHELBURGAS GDNS
OLD ON
ETHELBURGAS
EVELYN CT

BARBERRY

PENNY POT LANE OR ROUGH ROAD

ARMY FOUNDATION COLLEGE HARROGATE

PENNY POT LANE

PENNY POT LANE

Oakdale

OAKDALE MANOR

Rifle Range

Playing Fields

Bardner Wood

Running Track

Oakdale Farm

CORNWALL KENT

Long Crag

Little Wood

Oak Beck

Birk Crag

Birk Crag House

Dales Way Link

Pot Bridge Farm

The Oatlands

Nursery

Harrogate Arms P.H.

CRAG

Cardale Woodland

Harlow Carr Botanical Gardens & Museum

The Pi

LANE

ROAD

Keeper's Cottage

Cricket Grnd

HEAD ROAD

Crick Grnd

CAF

CARDAL

Cricket Ground

CARDALE P BUSINES PARK

Hotel

B6161

OTLEY

B6162

HOWHILL ROAD

BECKWITH HEAD

MOOR PK CL

School

Jackl

A **B** **C** **D**

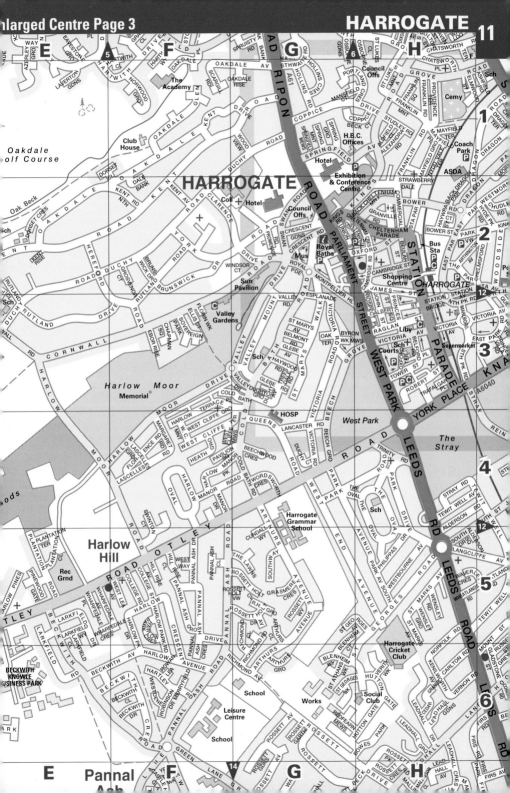

E 7 F G 8 H

Forest Lane Head
Liby
School
AVENUE
ALBERT PL
A59
CAMWAL
RD
BECK
SPA RD
BROUGHTON
SYCAMORE DR
GRO
PROSPECT
ROAD

MOORLAND RD
MOORLAND
VW
MOORLAND
CL
Knaresborough Round
WENTWORTH
WORTH
WENTWORTH
FOREST
CRES
FORREST HOUSE
FOREST
AVENUE
FOREST RISE
FOREST
FORE ST GRO
WAYZ
FAIRWAYS
FAIRWAYS
FAIRWAYS
FAIRWAYS
DRIVE
AVENUE
LINKS CL
LINKS W
AV

CASS LANE
C A S S
BELMONT AV
CALCUTT ROAD
BL
WHITE
HEAT
CORONATION TER
1

Starbeck
Bakery
FIELDS AV
FIRST AV
FOREST GDNS
CROSSWAYS
CRES
CROSSWAYS
HOOKSTONE PK
HOOKSTONE WY

Stoneface Farm
Forest Moor
Nurseries
FOREST MOOR ROAD
FOREST MOOR DR
BELMONT AV
FOREST MOOR

8

Thistle Hill Nursing Home
2

PLUMPTON
RETAIL
PARK
HOOKSTONE
HOOKSTONE CT
GRANGE CT
GRANGE
HOOKSTONE WY
FIELDS
PLUMPTON PARK
PLUMPTON
AND ROAD
PLUMPTON
PK
School
ROTHBURY CL
SHERWOOD
DE LA MERE
CRES
KIEL DER
DALBY
DALBY
AV
OVAL
FOREST LANE
CRES

FOREST LANE
FOREST LANE

3

HOOKSTONE CL
HOOKSTONE
ROAD
PLUMPTON GRO
PLUMPTON WK
PLUMPTON CL
PLUMPTON
DRIVE
MANOR
RUDBECK CRES
BOWLAND CT
BOWLAND

Star Beck
Harrogate Ringway

W E T H E R B Y
Supermarket
Works
ROAD
Bilton Court
(Geoplan)
Cemetery &
Crematorium
**HARROGATE
BUSINESS
PARK**
FREEMANS
WY
FOREST LANE

A658

4

Rudfarlington
Farm

RUDDING LA
LANE
COLLINS
HILL

R O A D
HARROGATE RD
A661
A658
5

CRIMPLE
RUDDING
LANE

Rudding
Dower

Brown
Hill
PLOMPTON
ROAD

6

E 16 F G H
Hotel
The Carrs
A658

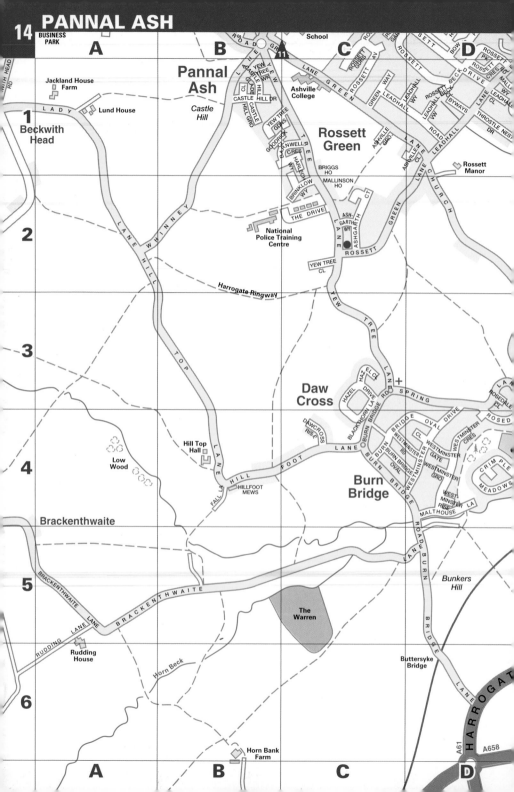

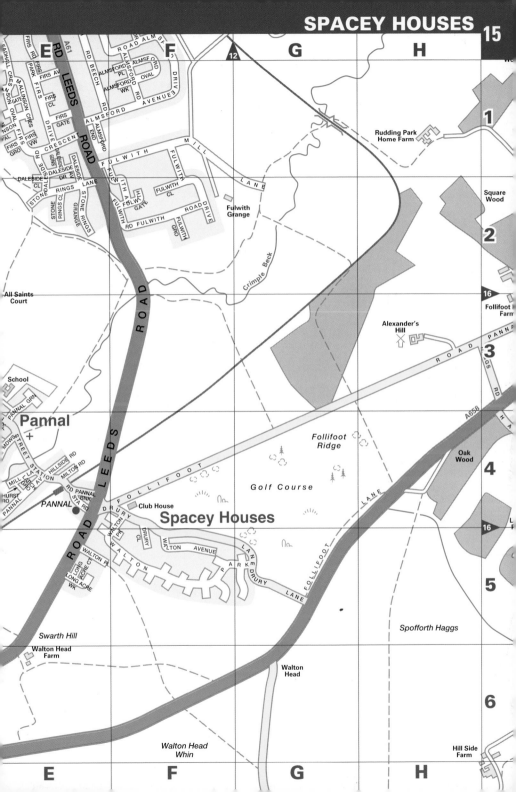

E **F** G **H**

12

Rudding Park
Home Farm

Square
Wood

1

2

16

Follifoot
Farm

ROAD ALM ST

FIRS RD A61
FADHALL CRES
FIRS
PARK FIRS
FIRS AV
M ALLINSON CRES
NSON GATE
OVAL FIRS VW
FIRS CL
FIRS GRO
FIRS GATE

BEECH RD
LEEDS
ROAD
CRESCENT
DALESIDE
STONEDALESIDE
DALESIDE DR W
DALESIDE
CL
DALESIDE

ALMSFORD
OVAL
ALMSFORD
WK
ALMSFORD
PL
ALMSFORD
AVENUE
ALMSFORD
END
ALMSFORD
RD

DRIVE

FULWITH
LANE
FULWITH
FULWITH
DR W
FOLW
GATE
FULWITH
RD FULWITH
FULWITH
GRO

MILL
LANE

FULWITH
CL
FULWITH
ROAD
DRIVE

Fulwith
Grange

STONE RINGS
RINGS
STONE
RINGS
GRANGE

Crimple Beck

All Saints
Court

Alexander's
Hill

ROAD
PANNA
GS
RD

3

A658

School

LEEDS

Pannal

PANNAL GRN
MDWS
STREET STATION RD
HILLSIDE RD
MILTON RD
PANNAL
BNK
PANNAL
ST RD

ROAD

Follifoot
Ridge

Oak
Wood

4

MILL CLA
BOX AV
HURST
RD
PANNAL
PANNAL

Club House

Golf Course

FOLLIFOOT

LANE

16

Spacey Houses

WALTON PL
WALTON
LONG ACRE CL
LONG ACRE
LONG ACRE
WK

DRURY
DRURY
CL
WALTON
WALTON AVENUE
PARK
LANE
DRURY LANE

FOLLIFOOT
LANE

5

Swarth Hill

Spofforth Haggs

Walton Head
Farm

Walton
Head

6

*Walton Head
Whin*

Hill Side
Farm

E **F** G **H**

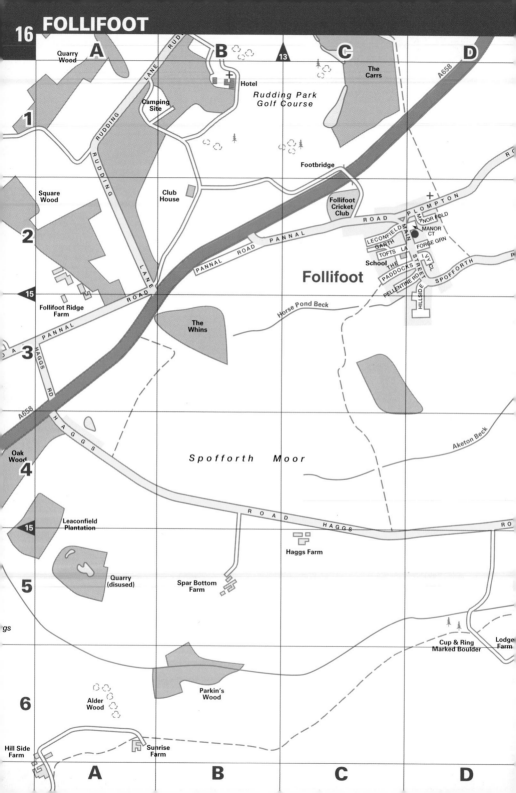

Quarry Wood

A

RUDDING LANE

B

13

C

The Carrs

D

A658

Hotel

Camping Site

Rudding Park Golf Course

1

RUDDING LANE

Square Wood

Club House

Footbridge

Follifoot Cricket Club

PLOMPTON ROAD

ROAD

LECONFIELD GARTH

NOR FOLD

MANOR CT

MAIN STREET

IVY CL

FORGE GRN

2

PANNAL ROAD

PANNAL ROAD

TOFTS LA

THE PADDOCKS

School

Follifoot

SPOFFORTH

PELLENTINE RD

HILLSIDE

15

Follifoot Ridge Farm

PANNAL

HAGGS RD

The Whins

Horse Pond Beck

3

A658

HAGGS

Oak Wood

Spofforth   Moor

Aketon Beck

4

15

Leaconfield Plantation

ROAD

HAGGS

RO

Haggs Farm

Quarry (disused)

Spar Bottom Farm

Cup & Ring Marked Boulder

Lodge Farm

5

gs

Parkin's Wood

Alder Wood

6

Hill Side Farm

Sunrise Farm

A

B

C

D

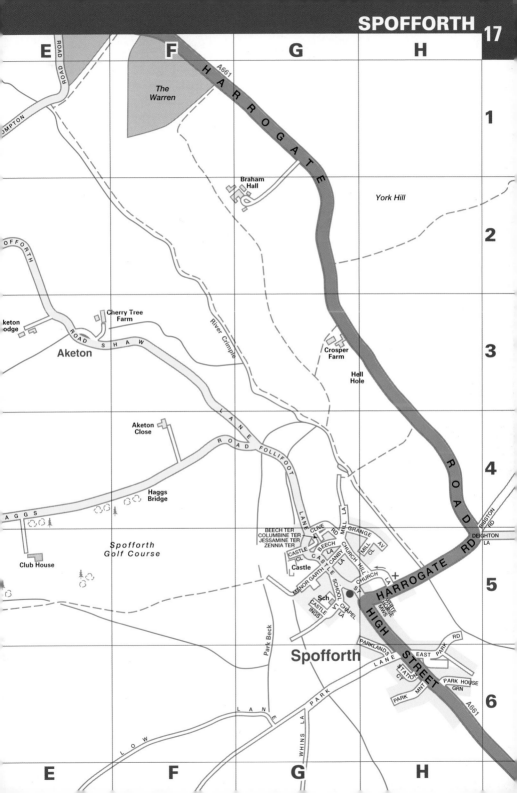

E | **F** | **G** | **H**

1
2
3
4
5
6

The Warren

A661

HARROGATE

Braham Hall

York Hill

OFFORTH

River Crimple

keton odge

Cherry Tree Farm

ROAD SHAW

Aketon

Crosper Farm

Hell Hole

Aketon Close

LANE FOLLIFOOT

ROAD

Haggs Bridge

AGGS

Spofforth Golf Course

Club House

Park Beck

BEECH TER
COLUMBINE TER
JESSAMINE TER
ZENNIA TER

CLIVE

CASTLE CL

Castle

BEECH LA

CAP LA

MANOR GARTH

CASTLE INGS

Sch

SCHOOL LA

CHAPEL ST

GRANGE

MILL LA

CANBY

CHURCH MILL LA

MILL CL

CHURCH

X

DEIGHTON LA

PRESTON RD

HARROGATE RD

ROAD

WHITE HORSE MWS

HIGH STREET

Spofforth

PARKLANDS LANE

STATION CT

EAST PARK

PARK RD

PARK MNT

PARK HOUSE GRN

LOW LANE

PARK LANE

WHINS LA

A661

The Index includes some names for which there is insufficient space on the maps. These names are indicated by an * and are followed by the nearest adjoining thoroughfare.

Frogmire Rd HG5 8 C2
Fulwith Av HG2 15 E1
Fulwith Cl HG2 15 F2
Fulwith Dr HG2 15 F1
Fulwith Gate HG2 15 F2
Fulwith Gro HG2 15 F2
Fulwith Mill La HG2 15 E1
Fulwith Rd HG2 15 F2
Gaker Walk HG5 7 H2
Garden Ct HG3 4 C3
Garsdale Rd HG5 8 D3
Gascoigne Cres HG1 12 B1
Gentian Glade HG3 11 E1
Gladstone St HG2 12 A6
Glebe Av HG2 3 A5
Glebe Rd HG2 3 A6
Glendowne Ter HG1 5 H5
Globe St HG2 12 D2
Goodrick Cl HG2 14 B1
Gordale Mnt HG5 8 D3
Gordon Av HG1 6 B4
Gracious St HG5 8 B4
Grainbeck La HG3 5 F3
Granby Pk HG1 12 B1
Granby Rd HG1 12 B2
Grange Av, Harrogate HG1 6 B6
Grange Av, Spofforth HG3 17 G5
Grantley Dr HG3 5 F6
Grantley Pl HG3 5 G6
Granville Rd HG1 3 B3
Grasmere Cres HG2 11 G5
Great Yorkshire Show Grnd HG2 12 D4
Green Dragon Yd*, Castle Gate HG5 8 B4
Green La HG2 11 F6
Green Way HG2 14 C1
Greenfields Av HG2 13 E2
Greenfields Dr HG2 13 E2
Greenfields Rd HG2 13 E2
Greengate Dr HG5 8 B1
Greengate La HG5 8 B1
Greengate Vw HG5 8 C1
Grey St HG2 12 A6
Greystones Av HG3 4 D3
Grimbald Crag Cl HG5 9 E5
Grimbald Crag Way HG5 9 E5
Grimbald Rd HG5 8 D5
Grimbald Way HG5 9 E5
Grimbold Crag Rd HG5 9 E6
Grosvenor Rd HG1 11 F2
Grosvenor Gro HG1 6 C5
Grosvenor Rd HG1 6 C4
Grove Park Av HG1 6 C6
Grove Park Ct HG1 12 A1
Grove Park La HG1 12 A1
Grove Park Ter HG1 3 D1
Grove Park Vw HG1 6 C6
Grove Park Walk HG1 12 A1
Grove Rd HG1 3 C1
Grove St HG2 12 D1
Haggs Rd HG3 16 A4
Halfpenny Cl HG5 8 C1
Halfpenny La HG5 8 C1
Hall La HG1 6 B4
Halstead Rd HG2 12 A5
Hambleton Cl HG5 8 C3
Hambleton Ct HG5 8 C3
Hambleton Gro HG5 8 C3
Hambleton Rd HG5 6 C6
Hamilton Av HG2 12 A5
Hampsthwaite Rd HG1 3 A1
Harcourt Dr HG1 12 A2
Harcourt Rd HG1 3 D3
Harebell Cl HG3 5 E5
Harewood Rd HG3 5 G6
Hargrove Rd HG2 12 C2
Harlech Way HG2 14 C1
Harlow Av HG2 11 F6
Harlow Cres HG2 11 F5
Harlow Grange Pk HG2 10 D5
Harlow Manor Pk HG2 11 F4
Harlow Moor Dr HG2 11 F4
Harlow Moor Rd HG2 11 E3
Harlow Oval HG2 11 F4
Harlow Park Cres HG2 11 F5
Harlow Park Dr HG2 11 F5
Harlow Park Rd HG2 11 F5
Harlow Pines HG3 11 E5
Harlow Ter HG2 11 F4
Harlown Gro HG1 7 F6
Harrogate Bsns Pk HG2 13 E4
Harrogate Exhibition & Conference Centre HG1 3 B3
Harrogate Rd, Harrogate HG3 17 H5
Harrogate Rd, Knaresborough HG5 17 H5
Harrogate Rd, Spacey Houses HG3 14 D6
Hartley Rd HG1 11 F6

Hartwith Cl HG3 11 F1
Hartwith Dr HG3 11 E1
Hartwith Way HG3 11 F1
Havikil La HG5 7 E1
Havikil Pk HG5 7 E1
Hawes Rd HG1 12 C1
Hawthorn Av HG5 8 C2
Hay-a-Park HG5 8 D2
Haywood Rd HG2 3 A5
Haywra Ct HG1 3 C3
Haywra St HG1 3 C3
Hazel Cl HG3 14 C3
Hazel Dr HG3 14 C3
Hazelheads La HG5 8 C1
Heath Gro HG2 11 F4
Heather Way HG3 5 E5
Heathfield Dr HG5 8 C3
Hereford Rd HG1 11 E2
High Bond End HG5 8 A2
High Moor La, Knaresborough HG5 6 D1
High Moor La, Knaresborough HG5 7 F1
High St, Hampsthwaite HG3
High St, Harrogate HG2 13 E1
High St, Knaresborough HG5 8 B3
High St, Spofforth HG3 17 H5
Highbank Gro HG2 7 G6
Highgate Pk HG1 12 B1
Hill Bank Rd HG1 7 G6
Hill Foot La HG3 14 B4
Hill Rise Av HG2 11 F5
Hill Rise Cl HG2 11 F5
Hill Top Av HG1 6 A4
Hill Top Cl HG1 6 A5
Hill Top Cres HG1 6 A5
Hill Top Dr HG1 6 B5
Hill Top Gro HG1 6 B4
Hill Top La HG3 14 A2
Hill Top Mount HG1 6 A5
Hill Top Rd HG1 6 A5
Hill Top Rise HG1 6 B4
Hill Top Walk HG1 6 B5
Hillbank Gro HG1 7 F6
Hillbank Vw HG1 7 F6
Hillfoot Mews HG3 14 B4
Hillside HG3 16 D3
Hillside Rd HG3 15 E4
Hilton La HG5 8 B3
Hollins Cl HG3 4 B2
Hollins Cres HG1 3 A1
Hollins Ct HG1 3 A1
Hollins Hall HG3 4 C3
Hollins La HG3 4 B3
Hollins Mews HG1 3 A1
Hollins Rd HG1 3 A1
Holly Ct HG5 8 C3
Homestead Rd HG1 3 D5
Hookstone Av HG2 12 A6
Hookstone Chase HG2 12 D3
Hookstone Ct HG2 13 E3
Hookstone Dr HG2 12 B4
Hookstone Grange Ct HG2 13 E2
Hookstone Grange Way HG2 13 E2
Hookstone Oval HG2 12 D4
Hookstone Pk HG2 13 E2
Hookstone Rd HG2 12 A6
Hookstone Way HG2 13 F2
Hookstone Wood Rd HG2 12 C4
Hope St HG5 8 B4
Hornbeam Cres HG2 12 A5
Hornbeam Park Av HG2 12 B5
Hornbeam Park Oval HG2 12 B6
Hornbeam Pk HG2 12 B5
Hornbeam Sq East HG2 12 B5
Hornbeam Sq North HG2 12 B5
Hornbeam Sq South HG2 12 B6
Hornbeam Sq West HG2 12 B6
Howhill Rd HG3 10 B6
Hurstleigh Ter HG1 12 C2
Hutton Gate HG2 11 H6
Hyde Park Rd, Harrogate HG1 3 D3
Hyde Park Rd, Knaresborough HG5 8 C1
Iles La HG5 8 C4
Inman Gro HG5 8 C2
Inman Walk HG5 8 C1
Innisfree Cl HG2 12 C3
Ivy Cl HG3 16 D2
James St HG1 3 B4
Jenny Field Dr HG3 5 E6
Jervaulx Dr HG5 8 D6
Jesmond Rd HG1 12 C1
Jessamine Ter HG1 17 G5
Jockey La HG5 8 B3
John St HG1 3 B4

Juniper Way HG3 5 F6
Keats Walk HG1 6 C4
Kendal Rd HG1 12 C1
Kenilworth Av HG2 11 H6
Kenneth Yam Way HG2 12 B5
Kennion Ct HG2 12 D2
Kennion Rd HG2 12 D2
Kent Av HG1 11 F2
Kent Bank HG1 11 E2
Kent Dr HG1 11 F1
Kent Rd HG1 3 A1
Kent Rd North HG1 11 F2
Kent Rise HG1 11 E2
Kielder Oval HG2 13 F3
King Edwards Dr HG1 6 B5
King James Rd HG5 8 C4
Kings Rd, Harrogate HG1 3 B3
Kings Rd, Knaresborough HG5 8 D3
Kingsley Cl HG1 12 D1
Kingsley Dr HG1 12 B1
Kingsley Park Mews HG1 12 D1
Kingsley Park Rd HG1 12 D1
Kingsway HG1 3 D3
Kingsway Dr HG1 3 D4
Kirkgate HG5 8 B3
Kirkham Ct HG5 8 D5
Kirkham Gro HG1 6 C4
Kirkham Pl HG1 6 C5
Kirkham Rd HG1 6 C5
Kirkstone Rd HG1 12 C1
Knapping Hill HG1 6 A6
Knaresborough Rd HG2 3 D6
Knox Av HG1 5 H5
Knox Chase HG1 5 H4
Knox Cl HG1 6 A4
Knox Dr HG1 6 A4
Knox Gdns HG1 6 A4
Knox Gro HG1 6 A4
Knox La HG1 5 H3
Knox Mill Bank HG3 5 H3
Knox Mill Cl HG3 5 G3
Knox Mill La HG3 5 G4
Knox Pk HG3 5 G3
Knox Rd HG1 6 A4
Knox Rise HG1 5 H5
Knox Way HG1 6 A5
Laburnum Gro HG1 6 C5
Lady La HG3 14 A1
Lancaster Park Rd HG2 12 C2
Lancaster Rd HG2,3 3 A6
Lands La HG5 7 H3
Langcliffe Av HG2 11 H5
Langcliffe Av East HG2 12 A1
Larch Gro HG2 15 E4
Larkfield Cl HG2 11 E5
Larkfield Dr HG2 11 E5
Larkfield Rd HG2 11 E5
Larkfield Way HG2 11 E5
Larkspur Gro HG3 11 E5
Lascelles Gro HG2 11 F4
Lascelles Rd HG2 11 F4
Laundry Rd HG1 7 F6
Laura Ct HG5 8 C3
Laurel Gdns HG1 12 D1
Laverton Gdns HG3 11 E5
Leadhall Cl HG2 15 E1
Leadhall Cres HG2 11 H6
Leadhall Dr HG2 11 H6
Leadhall Gdns HG2 11 H6
Leadhall Gro HG2 11 H6
Leadhall La HG2 14 D1
Leadhall Vw HG2 14 D1
Leadhall Way HG2 14 D1
Leconfield Garth HG3 16 C2
Leeds Rd HG2 3 C6
Levens Cl HG3 4 D3
Levens Hall Pk HG3 4 D3
Leyland Cres HG2 12 C1
Leyland Rd HG2 12 C1
Lichfield Gro HG3 5 F6
Lilac Gro HG1 6 C5
Lime Gro HG2 12 A1
Lime St HG1 12 A1
Lincoln Gro HG3 5 F6
Lindrick Way HG3 5 F6
Links Cl HG2 13 F1
Links Way HG2 13 F1
Littlethorpe Cl HG3 5 F6
Littondale Av HG5 8 D3
Lodge Ct HG3 4 A1
Long Acre Ct HG3 15 E5
Long Acre Walk HG5 15 E5
Long Crag Vw HG5 10 C1
Low La HG5 17 F6
Lund La HG3 4 C3
Lunedale Av HG5 8 D3
Lynton Gdns HG1 12 B2
Mafeking St HG1 6 C6
Main St, Follifoot HG3 16 C2

Main St, Pannal HG3 15 E3
Malden Rd HG1 12 C1
Malham Way HG5 8 D3
Mallinson Cl HG2 14 D1
Mallinson Cres HG2 15 E1
Mallinson Gate HG2 15 E1
Mallinson Gro HG2 15 E1
Mallinson Ho HG2 14 C2
Mallinson Oval HG2 15 E1
Mallinson Way HG2 14 D1
Malthouse La HG3 14 D4
Maltkiln La HG3 5 F1
Manor Cres HG5 8 C3
Manor Ct, Harrogate HG3 16 D2
Manor Ct, Knaresborough HG5 8 C4
Manor Dr, Harrogate HG2 11 F4
Manor Dr, Knaresborough HG5 8 C3
Manor Fold HG3 16 D2
Manor Garth HG3 17 G5
Manor Gdns HG1 5 F2
Manor Orchards HG5 8 C4
Manor Rd, Harrogate HG1 11 F4
Manor Rd, Killinghall HG3 5 F2
Manor Rd, Knaresborough HG5 8 C4
Manse La Ind Est HG5 9 E4
Manse La HG5 8 D4
Mansfield Ct HG1 3 B1
Maple Cl HG2 7 G6
Margaret Rd HG2 11 F4
Markenfield Rd HG2 5 G6
Market Pl, Harrogate HG1 3 C4
Market Pl, Knaresborough HG5 8 B4
Marlborough Rd HG1 3 D4
Marvell Rise HG2 6 B4
Masefield Cl HG2 6 B3
Masham Cl HG2 12 D4
Masham Rd HG2 12 D4
Mayfield Gro, Harrogate HG1 3 C3
Mayfield Gro, Knaresborough HG5 8 D3
Mayfield Pl HG1 3 C2
Mayfield Ter HG1 3 C2
Meadow Cl HG3 4 A2
Meadow Dr HG1 6 C3
Meadow Gate HG1 6 B4
Meadow Rd HG5 8 B3
Meadow Rise HG1 6 B4
Meadow Vw HG1 6 B4
Meadow Way HG1 6 B4
Meadowcroft HG1 6 B4
Merryfield HG2 11 F6
Midgeley La HG5 9 H6
Mill Cl HG3 17 H5
Mill Gate HG1 5 H4
Mill La, Pannal HG3 15 E4
Mill La, Spofforth HG3 17 G5
Mill Rd HG5 9 G6
Millfield Glade HG2 7 G6
Milton Cl HG1 6 B3
Milton Rd HG3 15 E4
Mire Syke La HG5 7 E1
Mitre Ct HG2 12 B6
Monkswell Pk HG5 9 E5
Montpellier Cl HG2 3 A4
Montpellier Gdns HG1 3 A4
Montpellier Hill HG1 3 A4
Montpellier Par HG1 3 B4
Montpellier Sq HG1 3 B4
Montpellier St HG1 3 B4
Moor Cl HG3 5 F3
Moorland Cl HG2 13 F1
Moorland Rd HG2 7 G6
Moorland Vw HG2 13 F1
Mornington Cres HG1 3 D1
Mornington Ter HG1 3 D2
Mount Gdns HG2 12 A6
Mount Par HG1 3 C3
Mount St HG2 12 A6
Mowbray Sq HG1 12 A2
Myers Green La HG3 4 D2
Myrtle Rd HG1 12 A1
Myrtle Sq HG1 12 A2
Nesfield Cl HG5 5 H6
Netheredge Cl HG5 7 H3
Netheredge Dr HG5 7 H3
New Rd HG5 7 F1
Newby Cres HG3 5 G6
Newland Av HG2 12 B3
Newnham St HG2 12 C2
Newtondale Cl HG5 9 E3
Nidd Bank HG5 8 A2
Nidderdale Dr HG5 8 D4
Nidderdale Lodge Pk HG5 9 E4
Nightingale Dr HG1 12 D1
Nora Av HG5 8 C3
Norfolk Rd HG2 11 H6

North Lodge Av HG1 5 H5
North Park Rd HG1 3 C4
Norwich Dr HG3 5 F6
Norwood Cl HG5 8 C1
Norwood Ct HG5 8 B2
Norwood Gro HG3 11 F1
Nunnington Cres HG3 5 G5
Nydd Vale Ter HG1 3 C3
Oak Av HG1 10 B2
Oak Bank HG1 5 H6
Oak Beck Rd HG1 5 G5
Oak Beck Way HG1 5 D4
Oakdale HG1 5 D4
Oak Ter HG2 3 B5
Oakdale HG1 11 E2
Oakdale Av HG1 3 A1
Oakdale Glen HG1 11 F1
Oakdale Manor HG1 10 D2
Oakdale Rd HG1 11 F1
Oakdale Rise HG1 11 F1
Oaker Bank HG3 10 B2
Oatlands Dr HG2 12 A3
Old Barber HG1 6 A4
Old Chapel Cl HG3 10 C2
Old Trough Way HG1 6 A4
Olive Gro HG1 7 E6
Olive Walk HG1 7 E6
Olive Way HG1 7 E6
Omega St HG1 5 H5
Orchard Cl HG5 8 C1
Orchard Ct HG5 8 C4
Orchid Way HG3 5 E6
Osborne Cl HG1 3 B1
Osborne Gdns HG1 3 B1
Osborne Rd HG1 3 B1
Osborne Walk HG1 6 A6
Otley Rd, Harrogate HG2,3 11 F4
Otley Rd, Killinghall HG3 5 E5
Over Nidd HG1 6 A4
Oxford St HG1 3 B4
Oxford Ter HG1 3 C5
Pannal Ash Cl HG2 11 F5
Pannal Ash Cres HG2 11 F6
Pannal Ash Dr HG2 11 F5
Pannal Ash Gro HG2 11 F5
Pannal Ash Rd HG2 11 F5
Pannal Av HG2 15 E4
Pannal Bnk HG2 15 E4
Pannal Grn HG2 15 E4
Pannal Rd, Harrogate HG2 16 A3
Park Av, Harrogate HG2 11 G4
Park Av, Knaresborough HG5 8 B3
Park Av South HG2 11 H5
Park Chase HG5 12 A2
Park Cl HG5 8 B3
Park Crest HG5 8 B3
Park Dr, Harrogate HG2 11 H4
Park Dr, Knaresborough HG5 8 C3
Park Edge HG2 12 B4
Park Gate HG5 8 B1
Park Gro HG5 8 B1
Park House Grn, Harrogate HG1 5 H5
Park House Grn, Spofforth HG3 17 G6
Park La, Harrogate HG2 11 G6
Park La, Knaresborough HG5 8 D3
Park Mount HG3 17 H6
Park Par, Harrogate HG1 12 A2
Park Pl HG5 8 B4
Park Rd HG2 11 G4
Park Row HG5 8 B3
Park Sq HG5 8 B3
Park Vw HG1 3 D3
Park Way HG5 8 B1
Parklands HG3 17 H5
Parliament St HG1 3 B3
Pasture Cres HG5 8 C2
Pavilion Sq HG2 11 F4
Pearl St HG1 7 E6
Pecketts Holt HG1 6 A4
Pecketts Way HG1 6 A3
Peckfield Cl HG3 4 A2
Pellentine Rd HG3 10 B2
Penny Pot Gdns HG3 10 C2
Penny Pot La HG3 10 A2
Penny Royal Cl HG3 4 D6
Pennywort Gro HG3 5 E6
Petergate HG1 3 B4
Philippas Dr HG2 11 H5
Picking Croft La HG3 5 E3
Pine St HG1 7 E6
Pinewood Gate HG2 11 E5
Pinfold Cl HG5 8 C4
Plantation Cl HG2 11 E5
Plantation Rd HG2 11 E5

Street	Ref
Plantation Ter HG2	11 E5
Plompton Cl HG2	13 E3
Plompton Dr HG2	13 E3
Plompton Gro HG2	13 E3
Plompton Rd HG3	16 D2
Plompton Walk HG2	13 E3
Plompton Way HG2	13 E3
Plumpton Pk HG2	13 E3
Plumpton Retail Pk HG2	**13 E2**
Poplar Cres HG1	6 C5
Poplar Gro HG1	6 B5
Poplar Way HG1	6 C5
Portland Cres HG1	3 B1
Powell St HG1	6 C6
Preston Bottoms La HG5	7 H2
Primrose Cl HG3	10 C1
Prince of Wales Mansions HG1	3 C6
Princes Sq HG1	3 C4
Princes St HG1	3 C4
Princes Villa Ct HG1	3 D5
Princes Villa Rd HG1	3 D5
Princess Av HG5	8 C4
Princess Cl HG5	8 C4
Princess Dr HG5	8 C4
Princess Gro HG5	8 D4
Princess Mead HG5	9 H5
Princess Mount HG5	8 C4
Promenade La HG1	3 A3
Prospect Cl HG2	13 E2
Prospect Pl HG1	3 B4
Prospect Rd HG2	13 E1
Providence Ter HG1	3 C1
Pump Hill HG5	8 B3
Quarry La HG1	5 H5
Queen Ethelburgas Gdns HG3	10 C2
Queen Ethelburgas Pk HG3	10 C2
Queen Par HG1	3 D4
Queens Gate HG1	3 D4
Queens Rd, Harrogate HG2	3 A6
Queens Rd, Knaresborough HG5	8 D4
Raglan St HG1	3 B5
Railway Rd HG2	13 E5
Ravens Ct*, Knaresborough Rd HG1	12 D1
Raw Gap HG5	8 B3
Rawson St HG1	3 B3
Raydale Cl HG5	9 E4
Rayleigh Rd HG2	12 A5
Red Hill La HG5	7 G2
Redfearn Mews HG2	11 G6
Redhill Cl HG1	6 A4
Redhill Rd HG1	6 A5
Regent Av HG1	12 A1
Regent Cl HG1	3 D1
Regent Mount HG1	7 F6
Regent Par HG1	12 A1
Regent Pl HG1	7 F6
Regent St HG1	12 A1
Regent Ter HG1	12 A1
Richmond Av HG2	11 F6
Richmond Cl HG2	11 G6
Richmond Rd HG2	11 G6
Rievaulx Av HG5	8 D6
Rievaulx Cl HG5	8 D6
Rievaulx Ct HG5	8 D5
Ripley Dr HG1	5 H4
Ripley Rd HG5	6 C1
Ripley Way HG1	6 A4
Ripon Rd HG1,3	3 A1
Ripon Way HG1	5 H6
Robert St HG1	3 C6
Roberts Cres HG1	6 A6
Robinson Dr HG2	11 F6
Roche Av HG1	6 C4
Rogers Sq HG1	3 C5
Rosedale HG3	14 D4
Rosedale Cl HG3	14 D3
Rosehurst Gro HG3	15 E4
Roseville Av HG1	12 B2
Roseville Dr HG1	12 B2
Roseville Rd HG1	12 B1
Roseway HG1	6 B5
Rosewood Cres HG1	12 C1
Roslyn Rd HG1	12 B3
Rossett Av HG2	14 C1
Rossett Beck HG2	11 G6
Rossett Beck Cl HG2	14 D1
Rossett Cres HG2	14 D1
Rossett Dr HG2	11 G6
Rossett Garth HG2	14 C1
Rossett Gdns HG2	14 C1
Rossett Green La HG2	14 C2
Rossett Holt Av HG2	11 G5
Rossett Holt Cl HG2	11 G5
Rossett Holt Dr HG2	11 F5
Rossett Holt Gro HG2	11 G5
Rossett Holt Vw HG2	11 F5
Rossett Park Rd HG2	11 H6
Rossett Way HG2	11 G5
Rothbury Cl HG2	13 F3
Rough Rd HG3	10 B2
Rowanlea HG2	11 F6
Rowden La HG3	4 A3
Royal Bri HG2	3 D6
Royal Par HG1	3 A4
Rudbeck Cl HG2	13 E3
Rudbeck Cres HG2	13 E4
Rudbeck Dr HG2	13 E4
Rudding La, Brackenthwaite HG3	14 A6
Rudding La, Follifoot HG3	16 A1
Russell St HG2	12 A6
Rutland Cl HG1	11 E2
Rutland Dr HG1	11 E3
Rutland Rd HG1	11 F3
Rydal Rd HG1	12 C1
Saffron Mdw HG3	10 D1
St Andrews Av HG2	12 C2
St Andrews Gro HG2	12 C2
St Andrews Par HG2	12 C2
St Andrews Pl HG2	12 C2
St Andrews Rd HG2	12 C2
St Andrews Walk HG2	12 C2
St Athans Walk HG2	11 G6
St Catherines Rd HG2	12 B4
St Clements Rd HG2	12 B3
St Clements Rd South HG2	12 C3
St Georges Av HG2	11 G5
St Georges Rd HG2	11 H6
St Georges Walk HG2	11 G6
St Helens Rd HG2	12 B4
St Hildas Rd HG2	12 B4
St James Bsns & Retail Pk HG5	**9 E5**
St James Dr HG2	12 A4
St Johns Cres HG1	6 A5
St Johns Dr HG1	6 A5
St Johns Gro HG1	6 A5
St Johns Rd, Harrogate HG1	6 A5
St Johns Rd, Knaresborough HG5	7 F1
St Johns Walk HG1	6 A5
St Leonards Cl HG2	12 C4
St Leonards Oval HG2	12 C3
St Leonards Rd HG2	12 C3
St Lukes Cl HG1	3 B1
St Lukes Mount HG1	3 C1
St Margarets Cl HG5	8 B3
St Margarets Garth*, St Margarets Gdns HG5	8 B3
St Margarets Gdns HG5	8 B3
St Margarets Rd HG5	8 B3
St Marks Av HG2	11 H5
St Marys Av HG2	3 A5
St Marys Walk HG2	3 A5
St Nicholas Rd HG2	12 C3
St Patricks Way HG2	12 C2
St Roberts Gdns HG5	8 C5
St Roberts Mews HG1	3 C6
St Roberts Rd HG5	8 C5
St Ronans Cl HG2	12 B4
St Ronans Rd HG2	12 B4
St Winifreds Av HG2	12 B3
St Winifreds Av West HG2	12 B3
St Winifreds Cl HG2	12 B3
St Winifreds Rd HG2	12 B3
Salisbury Dr HG3	5 F6
Sallow Heath HG3	5 F6
Saltergate HG3	5 F6
Sandhill Cl HG1	6 C4
Sandhill Dr HG1	6 C4
Sandhill Way HG1	6 C4
Savage Yd HG5	8 B3
Scargill Rd HG1	11 F1
School La HG3	17 G5
Scotch George La HG5	8 B2
Scotton Ct HG5	7 E1
Scotton Dr HG5	7 F2
Scotton Gro HG5	7 F2
Scriven Rd HG5	8 B1
Sedley Cl HG1	6 B4
Shaw La HG3	17 F3
Shelley Ct HG1	6 B3
Sherwood Dr HG2	13 E3
Silver St HG5	8 B4
Silverfields Rd HG1	12 B2
Skipton Cres HG1	6 A5
Skipton Rd HG1,3	3 D1
Skipton St HG1	6 B6
Slingsby Av HG5	8 B2
Slingsby Cres HG1	12 B1
Somerset Rd HG2	3 A5
Sorrel Gro HG3	5 E6
South Beech Av HG2	13 E2
South Dr HG2	11 H5
South Park Rd HG1	3 D5
Southway HG2	11 G5
Sovereign Pk HG1	11 F3
Spa La HG2	13 E1
Spa Rd HG2	13 E1
Spa St HG2	13 E1
Speedwell Glade HG3	5 F6
Spencers Holt HG1	6 A3
Spencers Way HG1	6 A4
Spital Cft HG5	8 B5
Spofforth Rd HG2	16 D2
Spring Gro HG1	3 B2
Spring La HG3	14 C3
Spring Mount HG1	3 A2
Springfield Av HG1	3 A2
Springfield Mews HG1	3 A2
Spruisty Rd HG1	5 H6
Stanhope Dr HG2	12 C2
Station Av HG1	3 C4
Station Bri HG1	11 H3
Station Bridge HG1	3 C4
Station Ct HG3	17 H6
Station Par HG1	3 C3
Station Rd, Goldsborough HG5	9 H5
Station Rd, Harrogate HG3	15 E4
Station Rd, Knaresborough HG5	8 B3
Station Vw HG1	12 D1
Stephenson Cl HG5	8 B5
Stockdale Cl HG5	8 B4
Stockdale Walk HG5	8 B4
Stockwell Av HG5	8 B3
Stockwell Cres HG5	8 C3
Stockwell Dr HG5	8 B2
Stockwell Gro HG5	8 B2
Stockwell La HG5	8 C3
Stockwell Pl HG5	8 B2
Stockwell Rd HG5	8 B2
Stockwell Vw HG5	8 C2
Stokelake Rd HG1	3 D3
Stone Bramble HG3	10 D1
Stone Rings Cl HG2	15 E2
Stone Rings Grange HG2	15 E2
Stone Rings La HG2	15 E2
Stonebeck Av HG1	5 H6
Stonecrop Av HG3	4 D6
Stonecrop Dr HG3	5 E6
Stonefall Av HG2	12 D1
Stonefall Dr HG2	12 D2
Stonefall Mews HG2	12 D2
Stonefall Pl HG2	12 D2
Stonesdale Cl HG5	9 E4
Strawberry Dale HG1	3 C3
Strawberry Dale Av HG1	3 B3
Strawberry Dale Sq HG1	3 C3
Strawberry Dale Ter HG1	3 C2
Stray Ct HG1	3 D5
Stray Rd HG2	3 D6
Stray Rein HG2	3 D6
Stray Walk HG2	3 D6
Studley Rd HG1	3 C2
Sundew Heath HG3	10 D1
Sutton Grange Cl HG3	5 G6
Swan Rd HG1	3 A3
Swarcliffe Rd HG1	12 C1
Sweet Briar HG3	5 F6
Swinburne Cl HG1	6 B4
Swinton Ct HG2	11 F4
Sycamore Dr HG2	13 E2
Sykes Gro HG1	5 H5
Tannery Ct HG5	5 E5
Tansy Cl HG3	5 E5
Tansy Gro HG3	5 E5
Teasel Gro HG3	5 E6
Tennyson Av HG1	6 B4
Tentergate Av HG5	8 B2
Tentergate Cl HG5	8 B2
Tentergate Gdns HG5	8 A2
Tentergate La HG5	8 A2
Tentergate Rd HG5	8 B2
Tewit Well Av HG2	11 H4
Tewit Well Rd HG2	11 H4
The Avenue, Harrogate HG1	7 F6
The Avenue, Knaresborough HG5	8 B2
The Briars HG5	8 C2
The Chase HG5	9 E4
The Drive, Harrogate HG1	7 F6
The Drive, Yew Tree La HG2	14 C2
The Ginnel HG1	3 B4
The Grove HG1	12 A2
The Lawns HG2	11 G5
The Oval HG2	11 H4
The Paddock HG2	8 D4
The Paddocks HG3	16 C2
The Parade HG1	3 C4
The Spinney HG5	8 D3
The Square HG1	12 A1
Thistle Hill HG5	8 B6
Throstle Nest Dr HG2	14 D1
Timble Gro HG1	5 G6
Tofts La HG5	16 C2
Torrs Rd HG1	12 C1
Tower St HG1	3 C6
Trafalgar Ct HG1	3 C6
Trafalgar Pl HG1	3 C6
Trafalgar Rd HG1	3 C6
Treesdale Rd HG2	3 A6
Trefoil Cl HG3	5 E6
Trinity Rd HG2	11 H4
Truro Cres HG3	5 F6
Truro Rd HG3	5 F6
Tunstall Rd HG2	12 C2
Tyson Pl HG2	12 D2
Udale Cl HG5	8 D4
Union St, Harrogate HG1	3 B3
Union St, Knaresborough HG5	8 B4
Unity Cl HG1	6 A6
Unity Gro HG1	6 A6
Vale Ct HG5	8 A3
Valley Dr HG2	3 A5
Valley Mount HG2	3 A5
Valley Rd HG2	3 A4
Verity Walk HG2	11 H6
Vernon Rd HG2	11 H6
Vicarage La HG5	8 B3
Victoria Av, Harrogate HG1	3 B5
Victoria Av, Knaresborough HG5	8 B1
Victoria Cl HG1	3 D5
Victoria Mews HG2	3 A6
Victoria Rd HG2	3 A6
Victoria Shopping Centre HG1	**3 C4**
Victoria Ter HG1	7 F6
Wainfleet Rd HG1	6 A4
Walnut Gro HG1	6 C5
Walton Av HG3	15 F5
Walton Pk HG3	15 F5
Walton Pl HG3	15 E5
Walworth Av HG2	12 D2
Warren Pl HG1	6 A5
Warwick Cres HG2	12 A4
Water Bag Bank HG5	8 A3
Water La HG5	8 C1
Waterloo St HG1	6 B6
Waterside HG5	8 B3
Waverley Cres HG2	11 H5
Wayside Av HG2	12 C3
Wayside Cl HG2	12 C3
Wayside Cres HG2	12 C3
Wayside Gro HG2	12 C3
Wayside Walk HG2	12 C3
Wedderburn Av HG2	12 D1
Wedderburn Cl HG2	12 D1
Wedderburn Dr HG2	12 D2
Wedderburn Lodge HG2	12 C3
Wedderburn Rd HG2	12 C3
Wellington St HG5	8 B4
Wensley Gro HG2	11 H5
Wensley Rd HG2	11 H5
Wentworth Cl HG2	13 E1
Wentworth Cres HG2	13 E1
West Cliffe Gro HG2	11 F4
West Cliffe Mews HG2	11 F4
West Cliffe Mount HG2	11 F4
West Cliffe Ter HG2	11 F4
West Ct HG3	4 C3
West End Av HG2	11 G4
West La HG3	4 A5
West Lea Av HG2	11 F5
West Pk HG1	3 B5
West St HG1	5 H5
West Way HG2	11 F5
Westbourne Av HG2	11 H5
Westdene HG2	11 F6
Westminster Cl HG3	14 D4
Westminster Cres HG3	14 D4
Westminster Dr HG3	14 D4
Westminster Gate HG3	14 D4
Westminster Gro HG3	14 D4
Westminster Rd HG3	14 C4
Westminster Rise HG3	14 D4
Westmoreland Pas HG1	3 D2
Westmoreland St HG1	3 D3
Westville Oval HG1	5 H5
Wetherby Rd, Harrogate HG2	12 B2
Wetherby Rd, Knaresborough HG5	8 D4
Wharfedale Av HG2	11 E5
Wharfedale Cres HG2	11 E5
Wharfedale Pl HG2	11 E5
Wheatlands Gro HG2	12 A5
Wheatlands Rd HG2	11 H5
Wheatlands Rd East HG2	12 A5
Wheatlands Way HG2	12 A4
Whincup Av HG5	8 B3
Whincup Cl HG5	8 B3
Whincup Gro HG5	8 B3
Whinney La HG3	14 A2
Whins La HG3	17 G6
White Horse Mews HG3	17 H5
Whiteway Head HG5	8 B5
Whitsundale Cl HG5	8 D4
Widdale Rd HG5	9 E4
Willaston Cres HG2	12 C2
Willaston Rd HG2	12 B2
Willow Gro HG1	6 B5
Windsor Ct HG1	11 F2
Windsor La HG5	8 B4
Windsor Rd HG2	12 C4
Winksley Gro HG3	5 F6
Winter Grn HG3	10 D1
Wood Aven Cl HG3	5 E6
Wood Park Cl HG2	12 D4
Wood Vw HG1	11 G1
Woodbine Ter HG1	3 C3
Woodcock Cl HG3	15 E4
Woodfield Av HG1	6 B6
Woodfield Dr HG1	6 C6
Woodfield Gdns HG1	6 B6
Woodfield Gro HG1	6 B6
Woodfield Pl HG1	6 B6
Woodfield Rd HG1	6 B6
Woodfield Sq HG1	6 B6
Woodhall Dr HG1	6 C4
Woodhall Gro HG1	6 C4
Woodlands Av HG2	12 D3
Woodlands Cl HG2	12 D3
Woodlands Cres HG2	12 D3
Woodlands Dr HG2	12 D3
Woodlands Grn HG2	12 C4
Woodlands Gro HG2	12 C4
Woodlands Rd HG2	12 D3
Woodlands Rise HG2	12 D3
Woodlands Walk HG2	13 E3
Woodpark Av HG5	9 H5
Woodpark Dr HG5	9 H5
Woodruff Cl HG3	5 F6
Woodside HG1	3 D4
Wordsworth Cres HG1	11 G4
Wreaks Rd HG1	12 D1
Yarrow Dr HG3	5 E6
Yew Tree Cl HG2	14 C2
Yew Tree Gdns HG2	14 B1
Yew Tree La HG2	14 B1
Yew Tree Walk HG2	14 B1
Yewdale Rd HG2	12 B4
York Cl HG5	8 C4
York Garth HG5	8 C4
York La HG5	8 C4
York Pl, Harrogate HG1	3 C6
York Pl, Knaresborough HG5	8 C4
York Rd, Harrogate HG1	3 A3
York Rd, Knaresborough HG5	8 C4
Youngs Dr HG3	10 C2
Zennia Ter HG3	17 G5